BullShit

An Irreverent Adult Coloring Book
For Release Anger

By

S.B. Nozaz

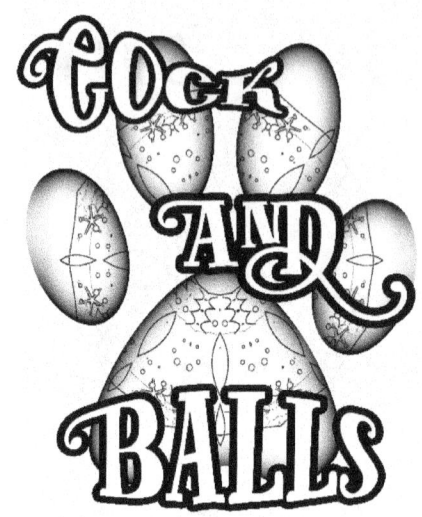

Copyright © 2016 by S.B. Nozaz

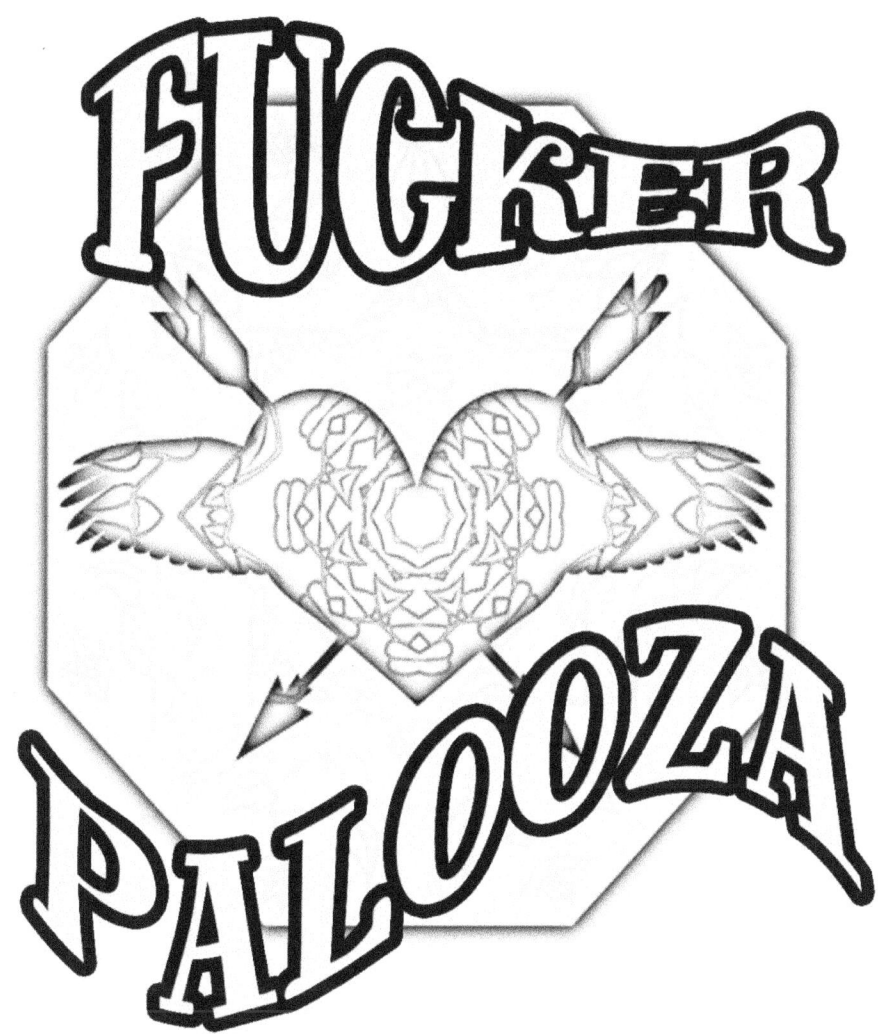

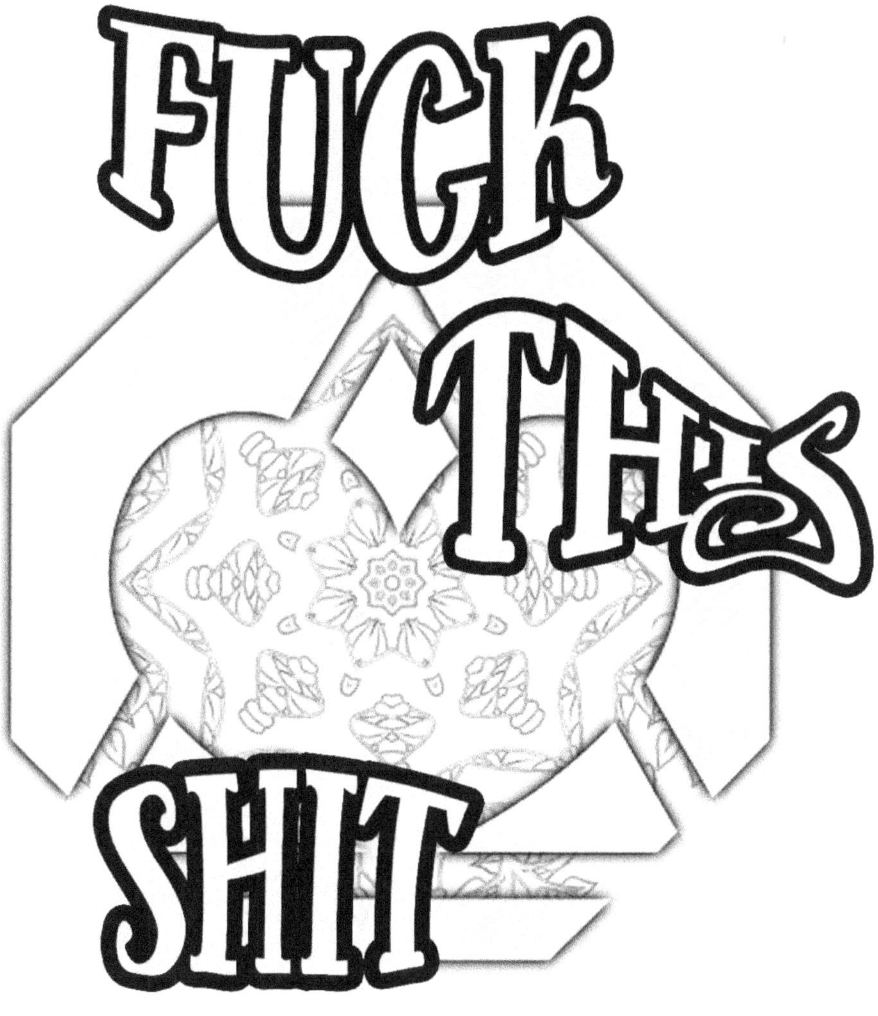
FUCK
THIS
SHIT

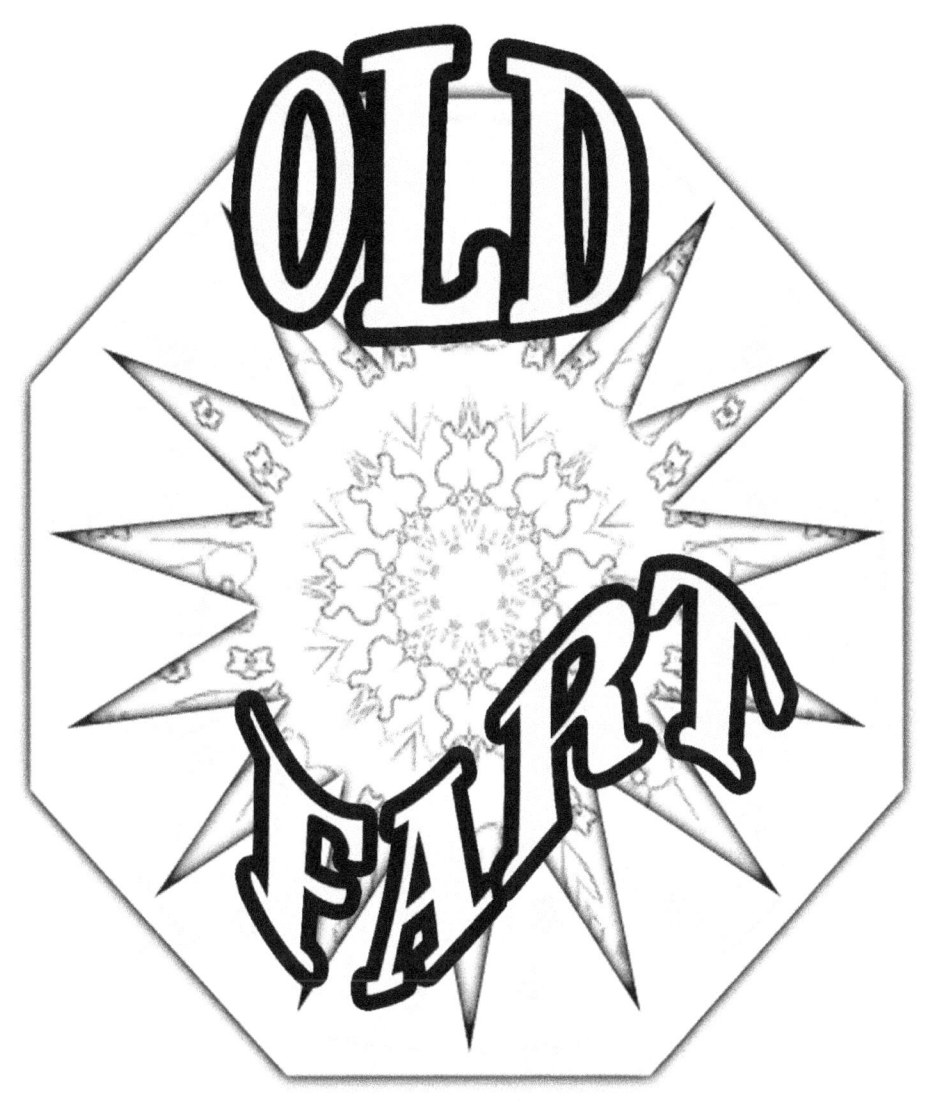

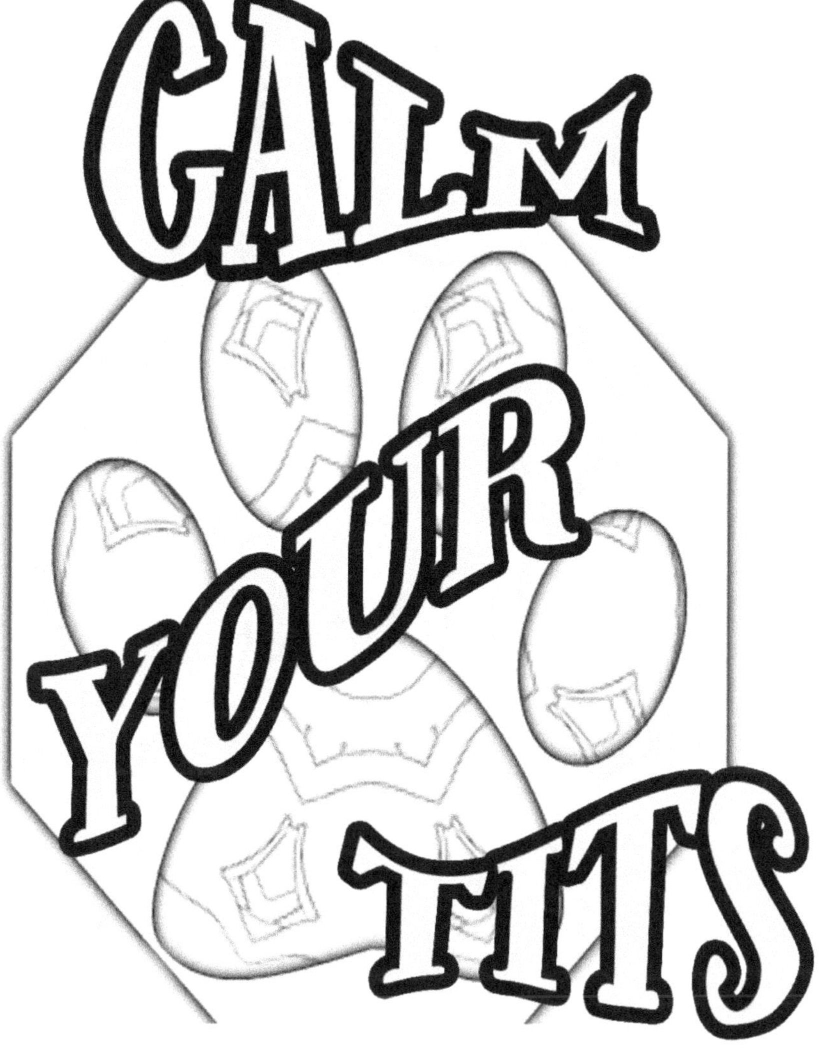
CALM
YOUR
TITS

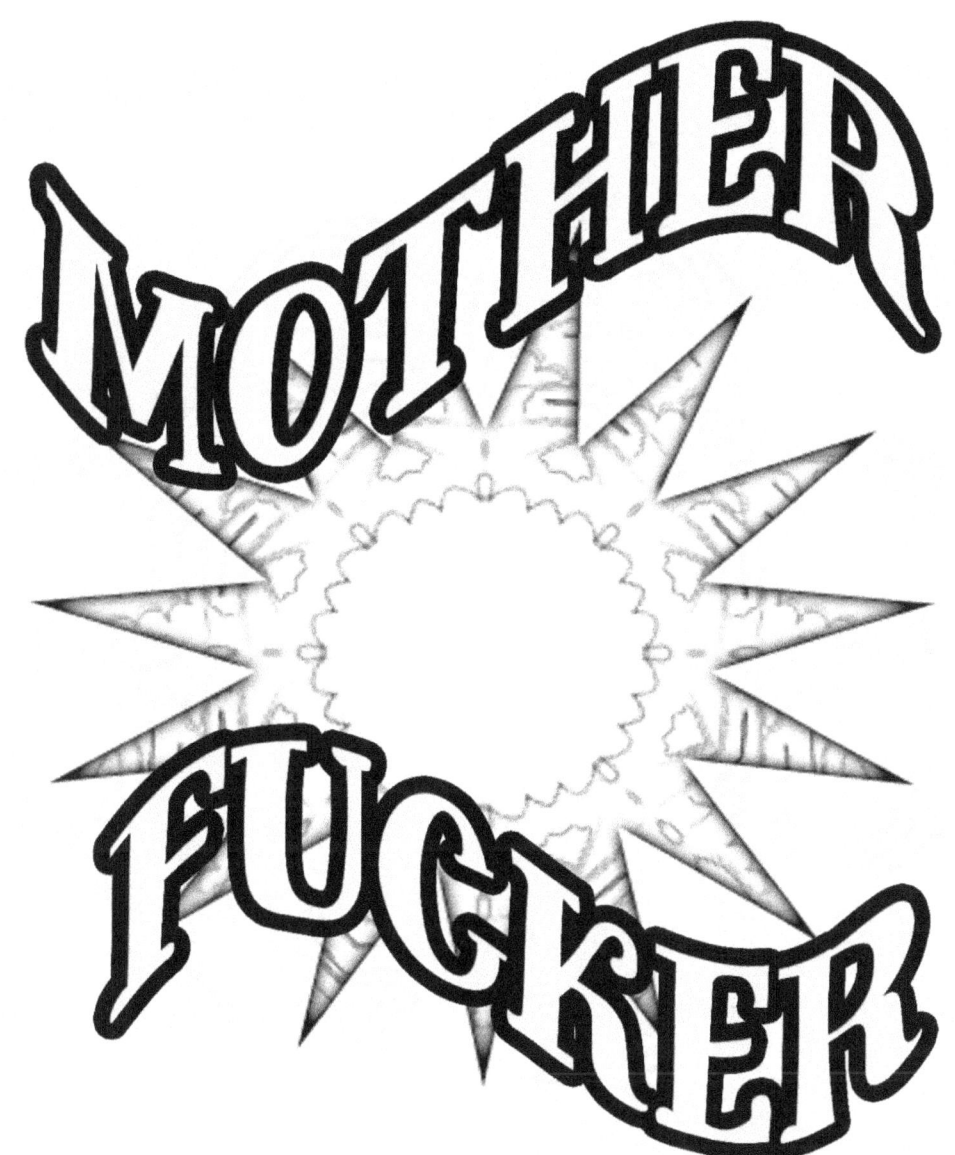

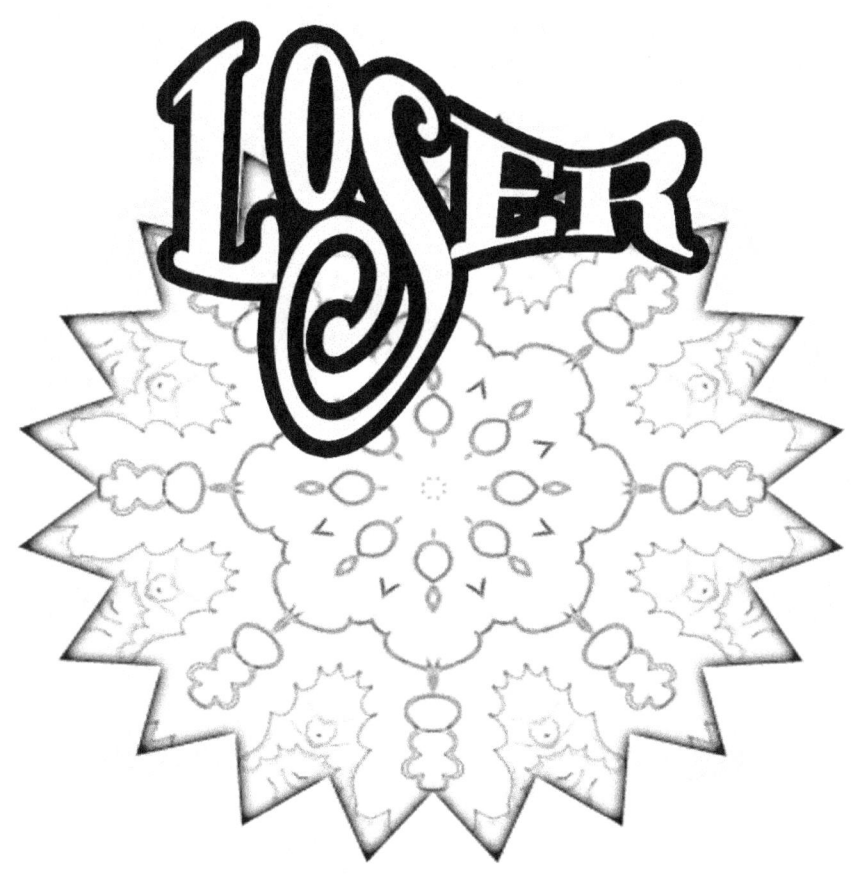

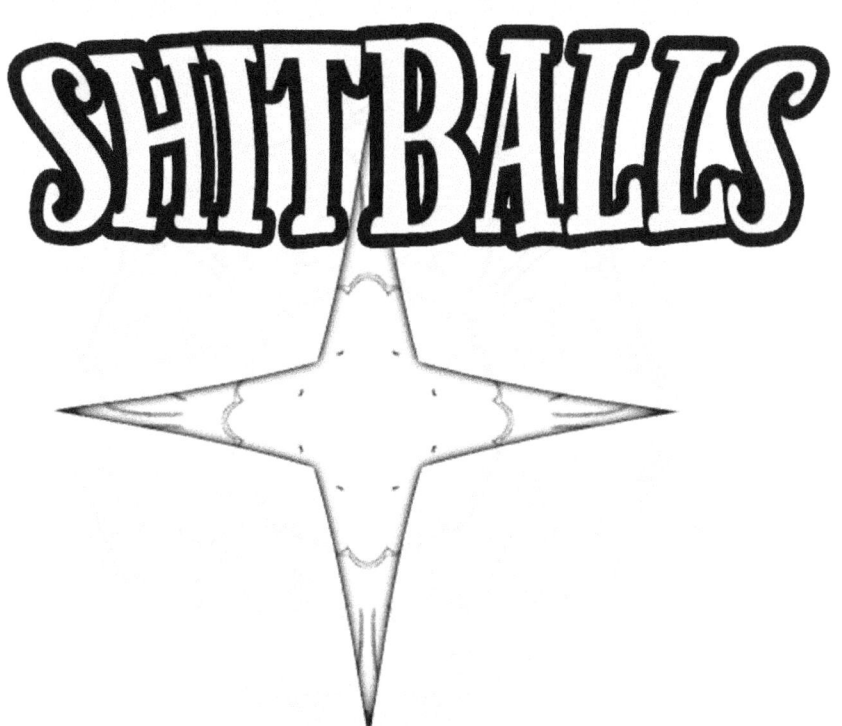

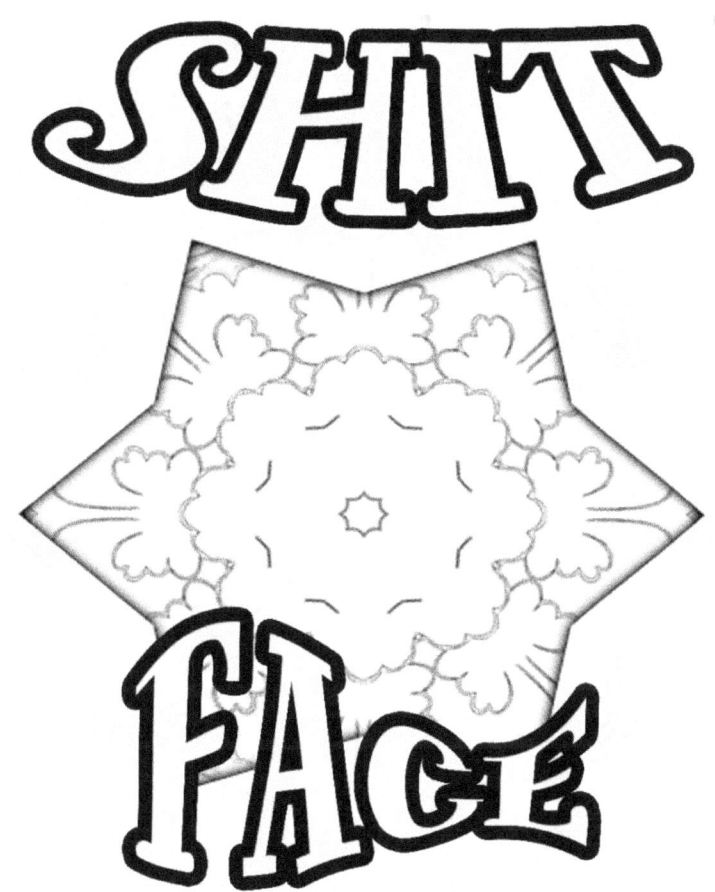

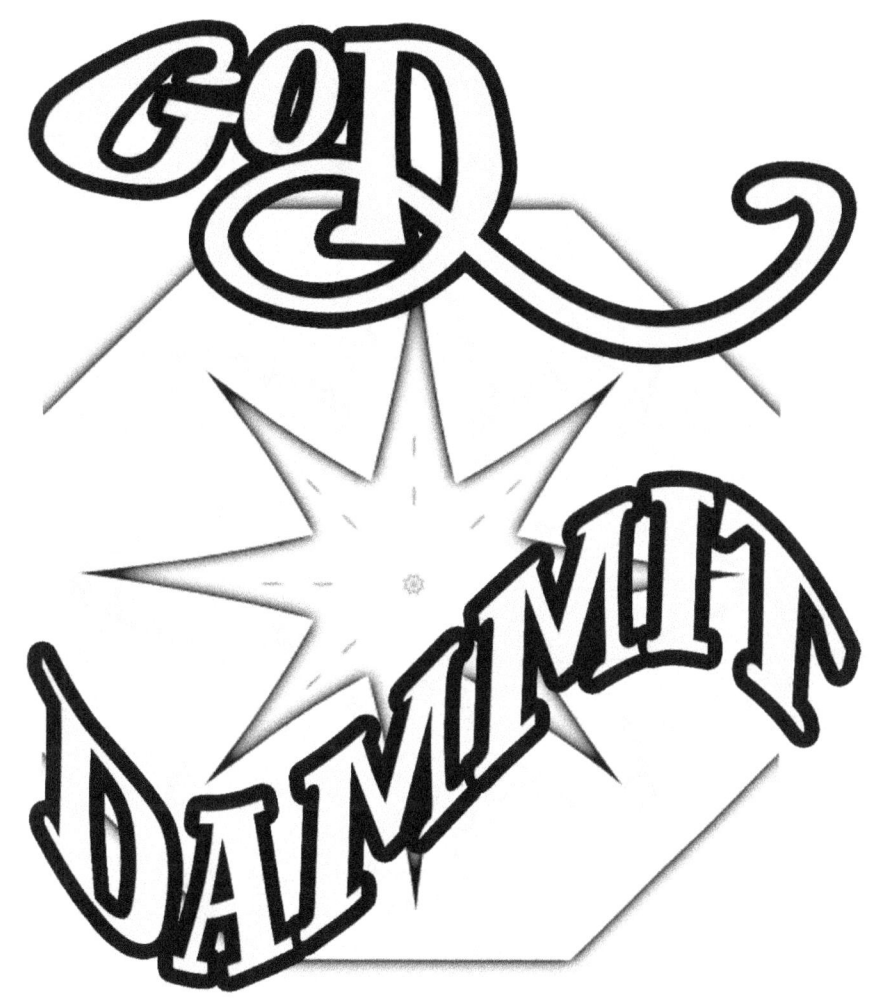

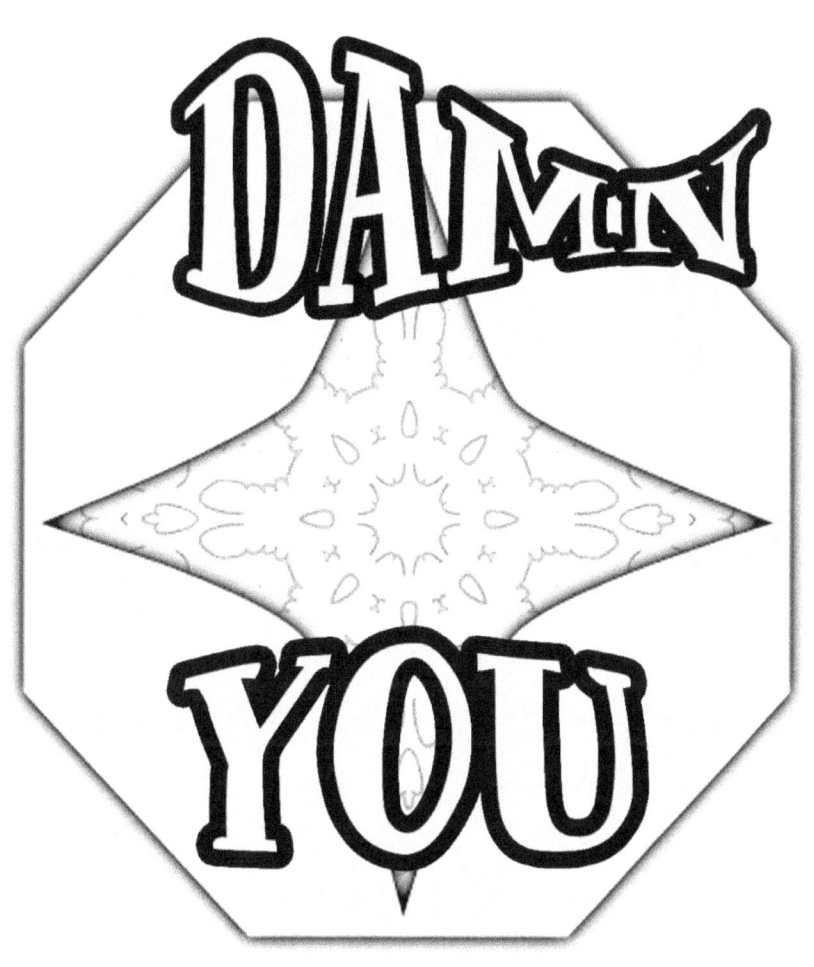

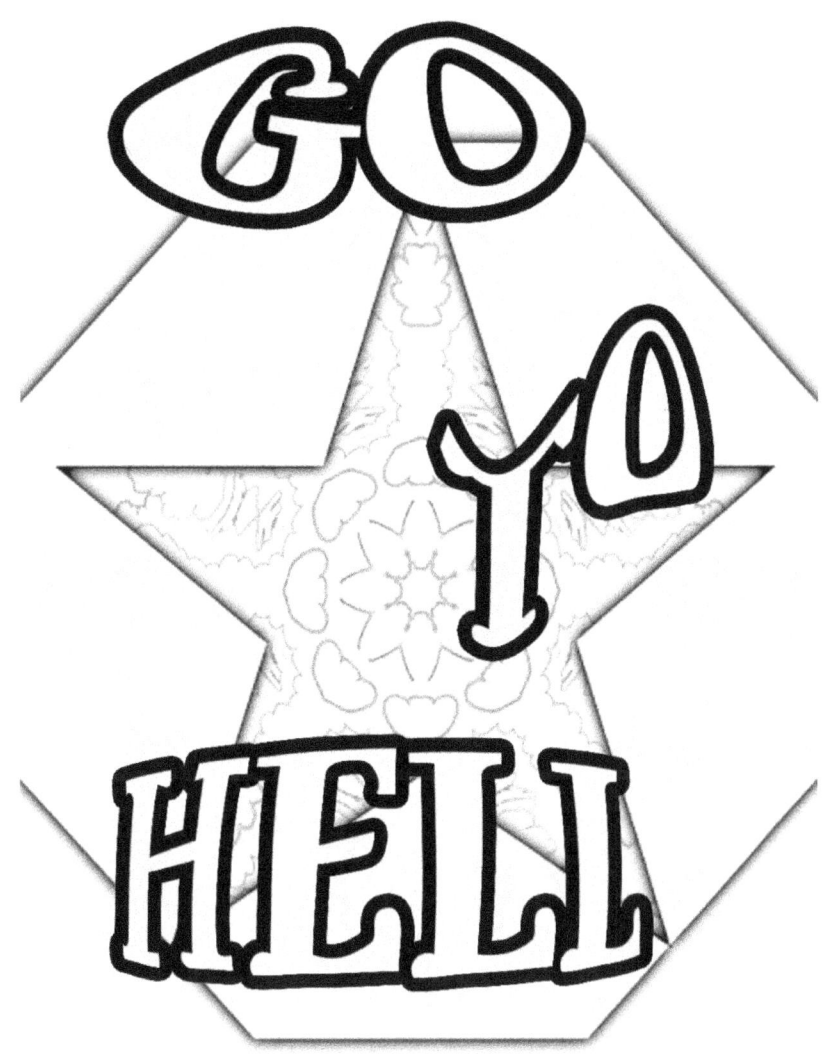

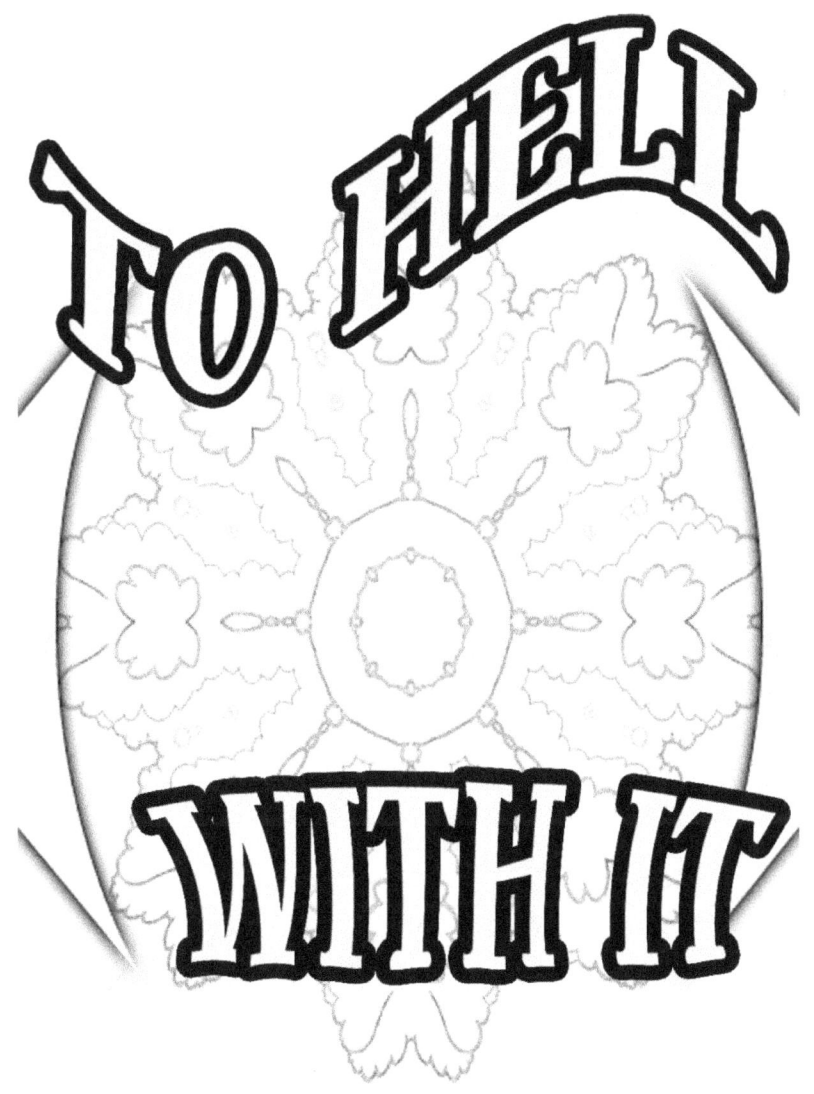

TO HELL WITH IT

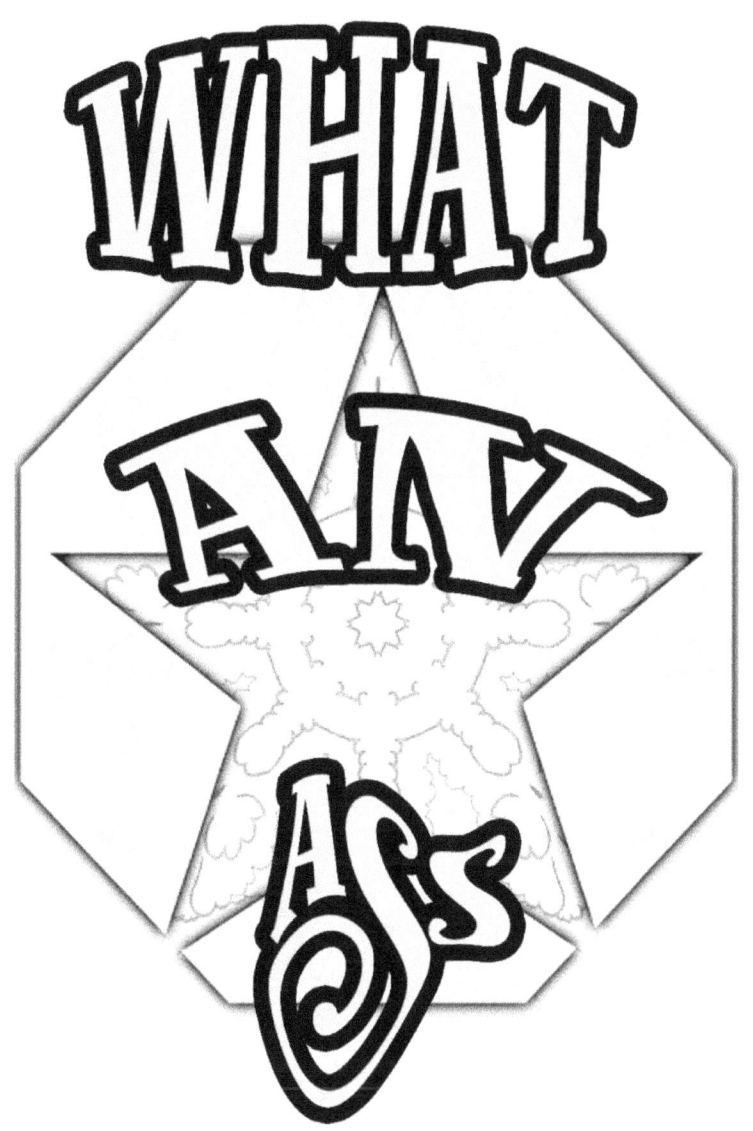

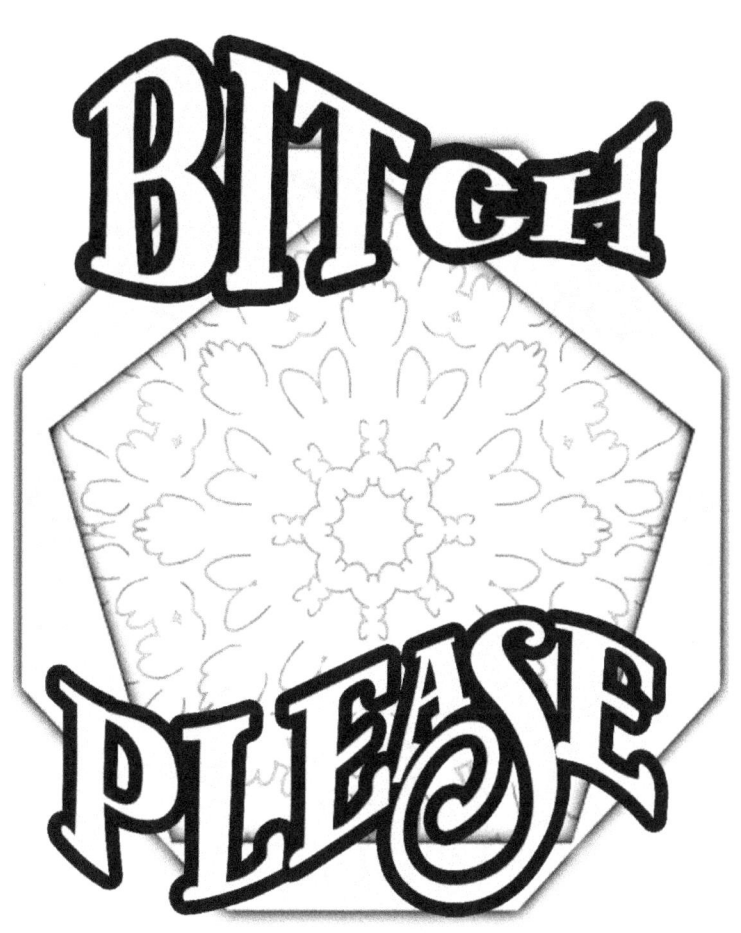

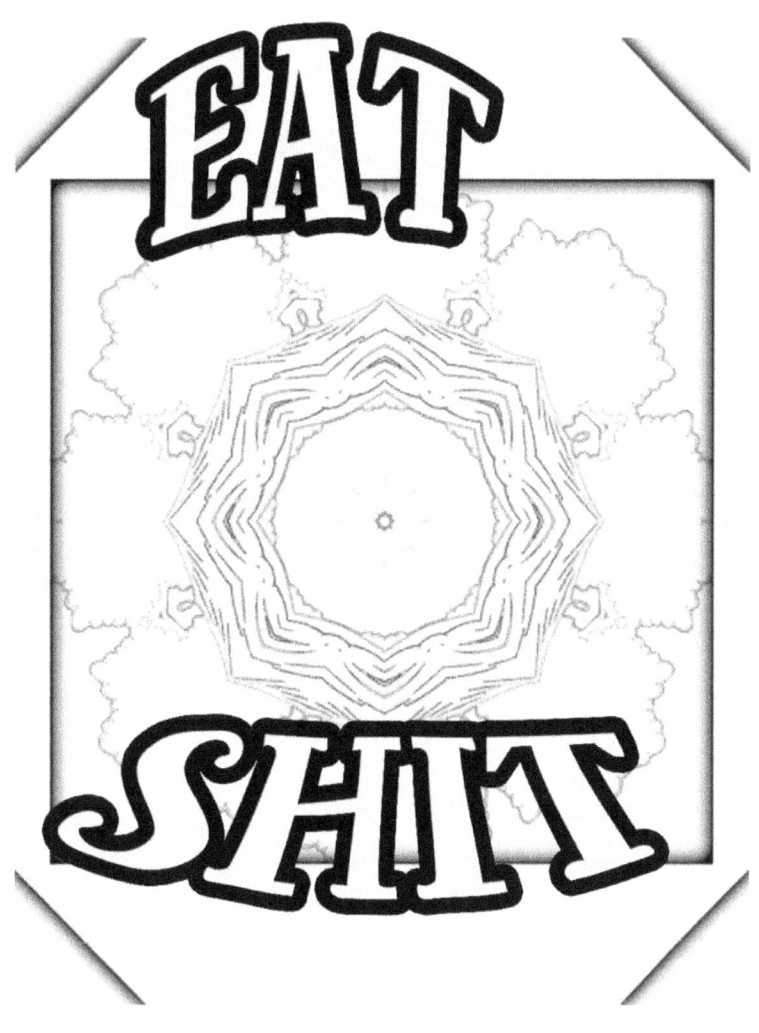

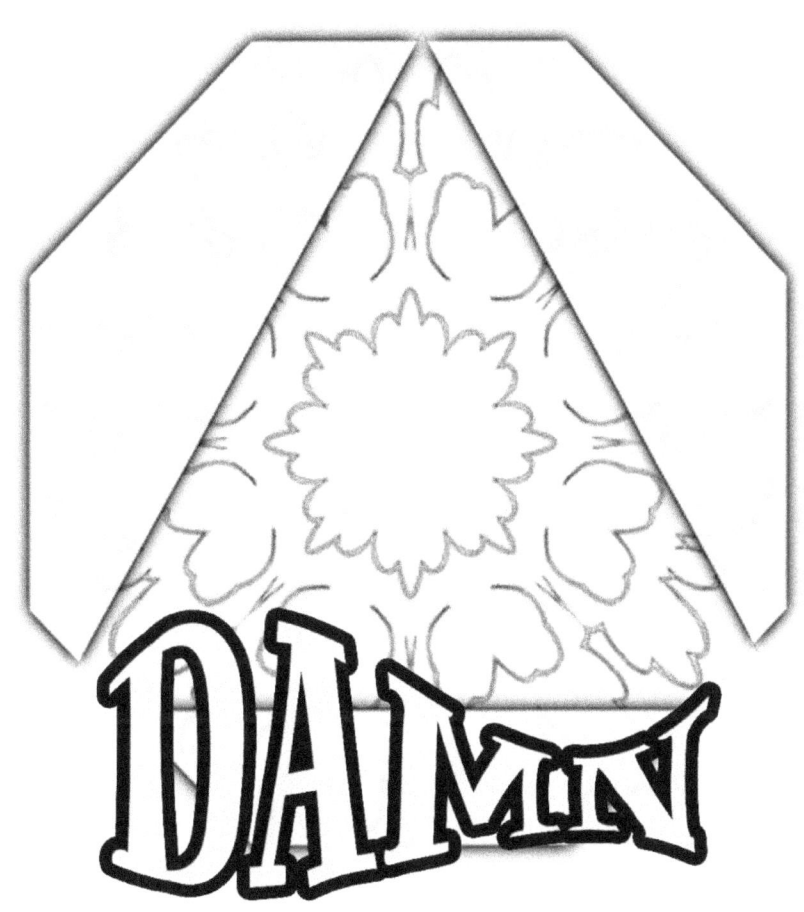

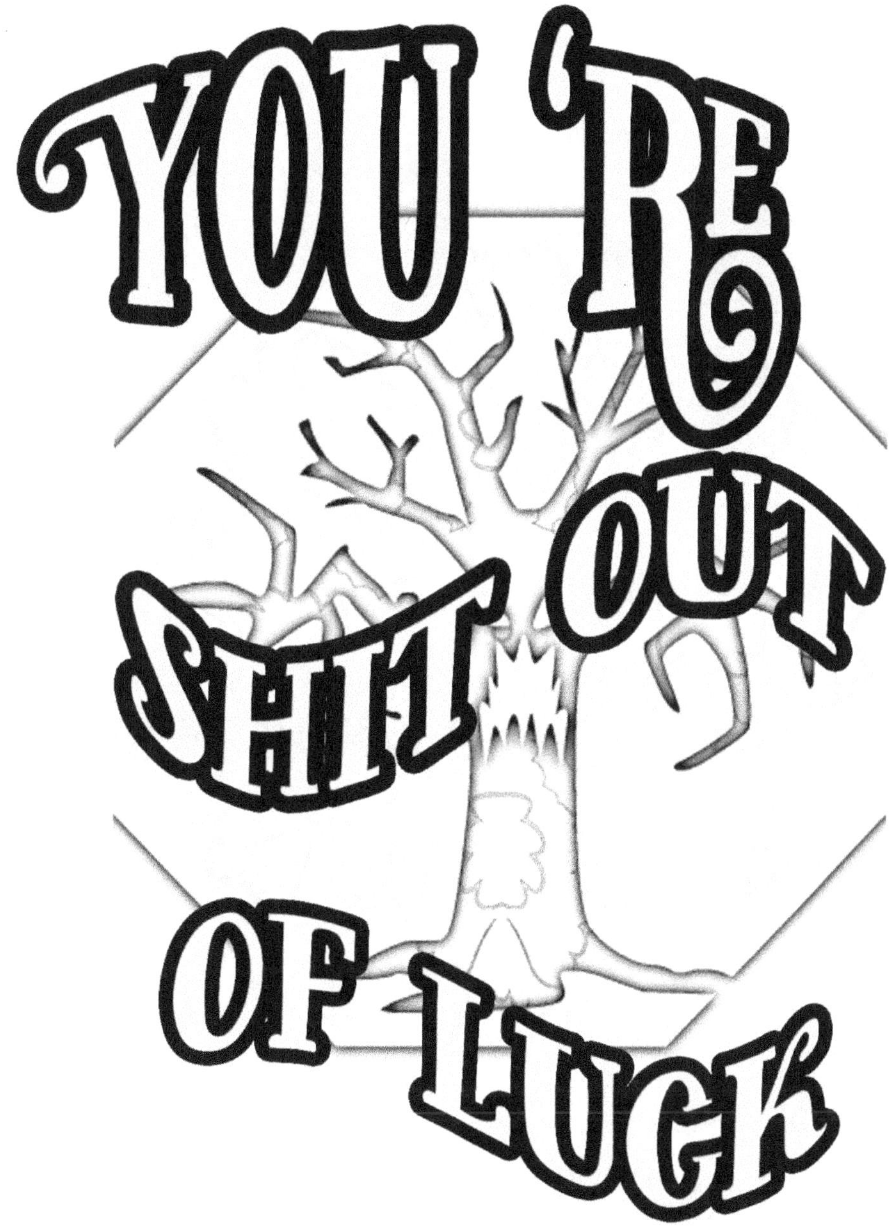
YOU 'RE
SHIT OUT
OF LUCK

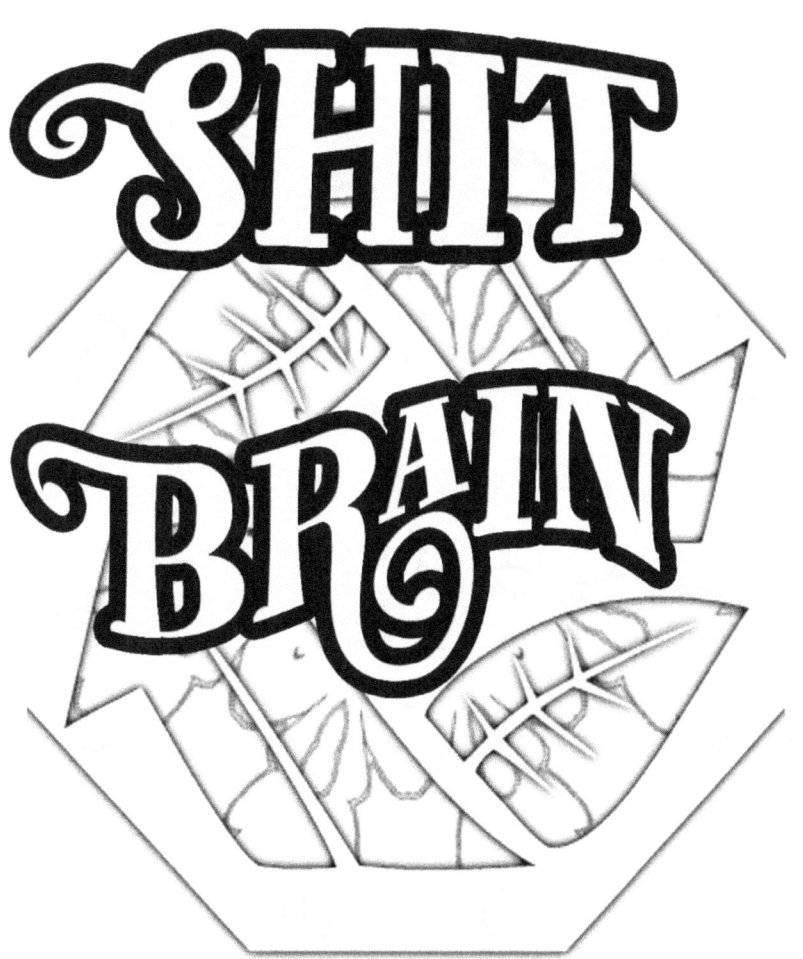

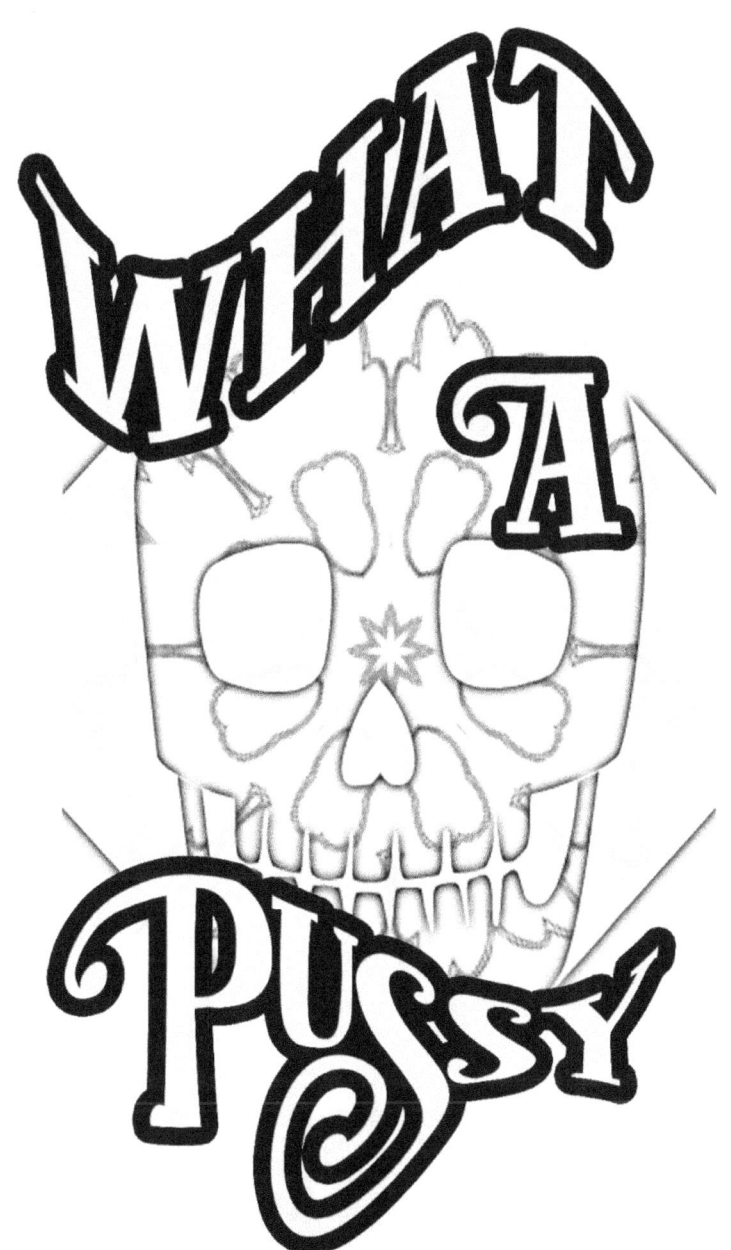

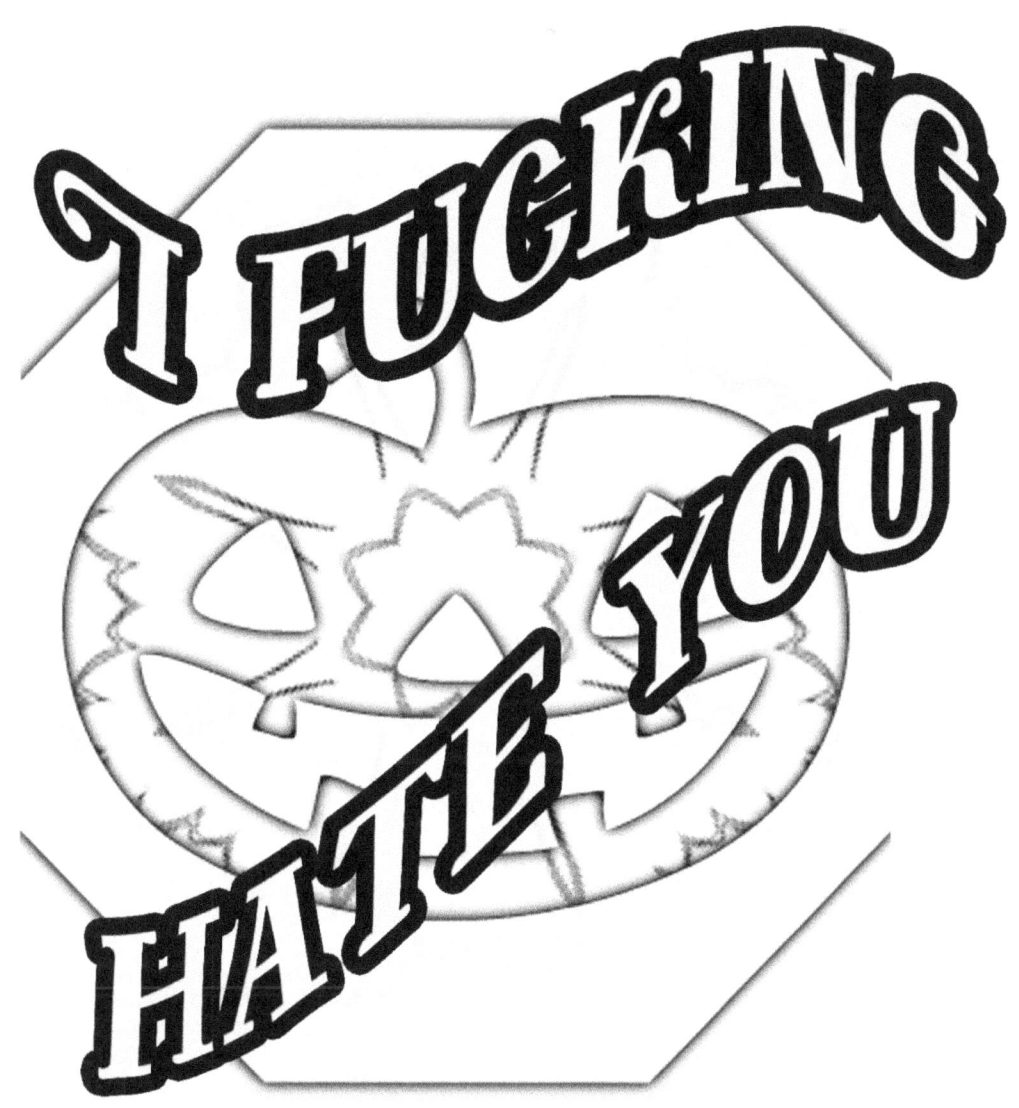

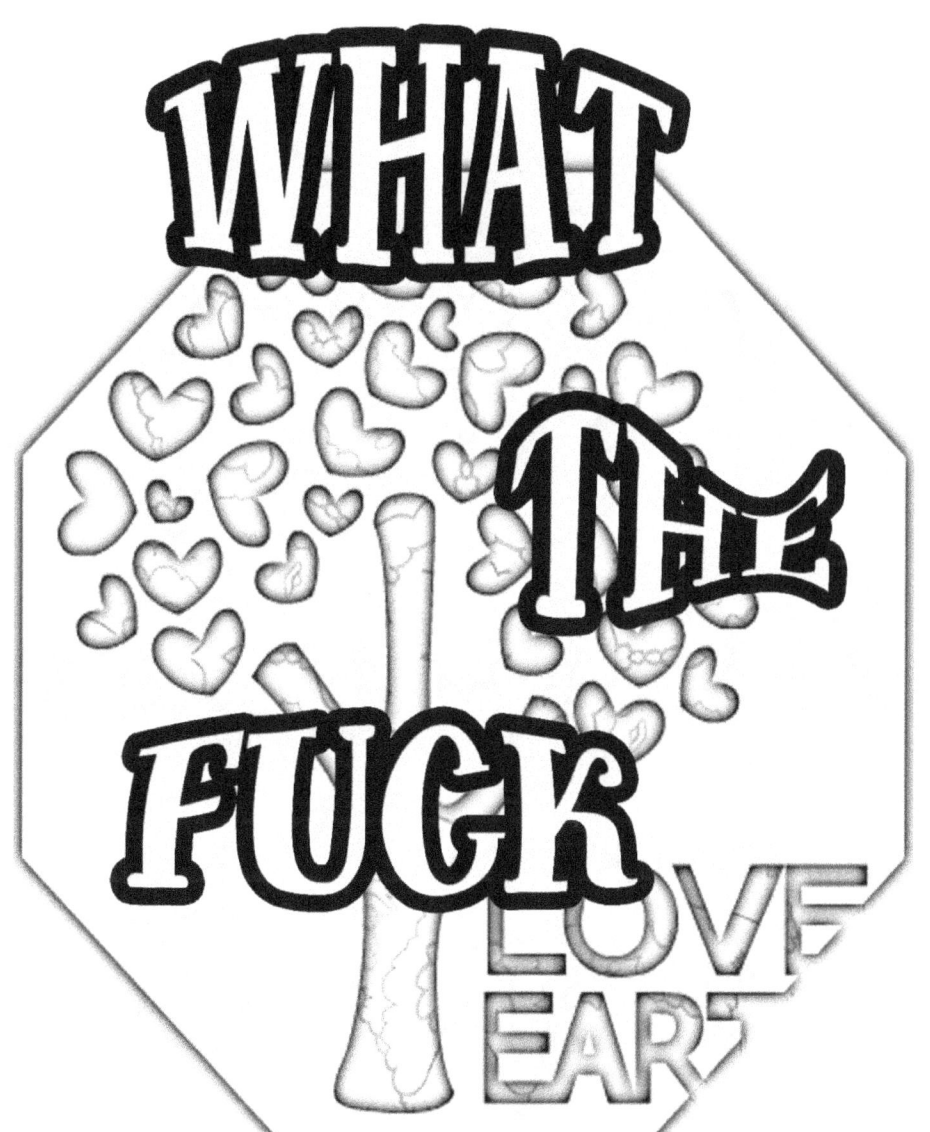

SON OF
A BITCH

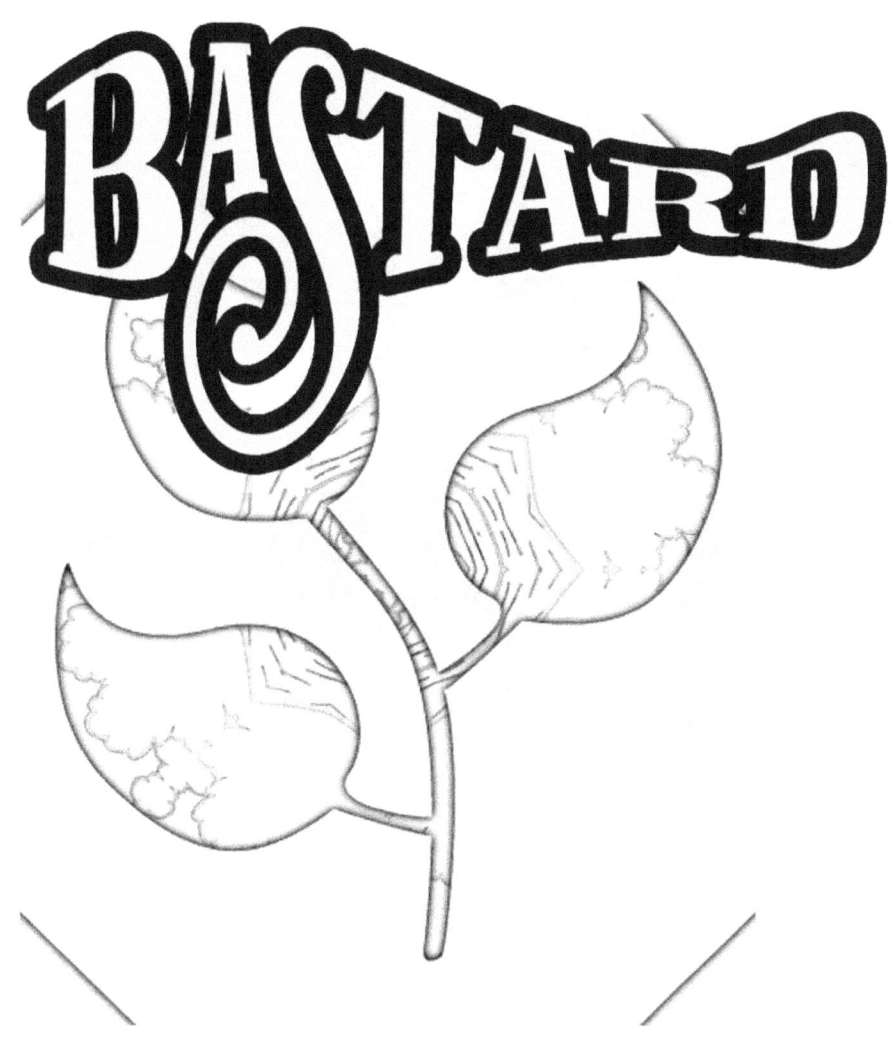

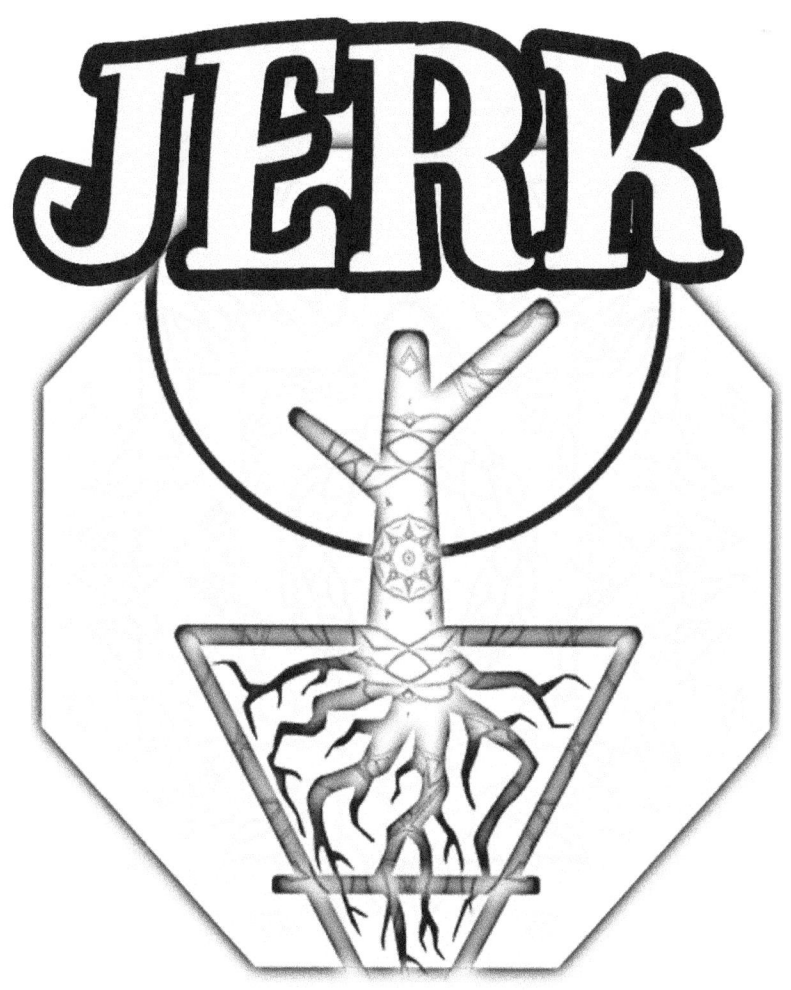

Note

www.ingramcontent.com/pod-product-compliance
Lightning Source LLC
Chambersburg PA
CBHW080638190526
45169CB00009B/3419